INSULTS
Every Man Should Know

Text copyright © 2011 by Quirk Productions, Inc.

Library of Congress Cataloging in Publication Number: 2011922697

ISBN: 978-1-59474-524-9

Printed in China

Typeset in Goudy and Monotype Old Style

Designed by Katie Hatz
Production management by John J. McGurk

Quirk Books
215 Church Street
Philadelphia, PA 19106
quirkbooks.com

10 9 8 7 6 5 4 3

INSULTS

Every Man Should Know

By Nick Mamatas

QUIRK BOOKS
PHILADELPHIA

The Greeks have a word for it. That word, most often, is *malaka*. Malaka is perhaps the most common utterance in Greece, and is used as constantly and as enthusiastically as the Smurfs used the word *smurf*. It is most frequently translated as "wanker"—British slang for "jerkoff-slash-douchebag"—but that fails to capture the true subtleties of the term. Really, a malaka is someone who has been so excessive in his masturbation that he has rendered himself brain-damaged. It's a perfect insult for men to use against other men, for it encapsulates all the anxieties that are part and parcel of masculinity: virility, sexuality, competence, and intelligence.

But malaka isn't just an insult for male targets. Machines, traffic jams, the thrust and parry of politicians, a dropped glass, a jammed rifle or printer, a recalcitrant donkey, the rate of inflation—all are malaka. And the actions of malakas are known as *malachies* (ma-la-chee-ehs). In the worldview of the Greek insult, the sorry state of life on Earth as well as all your personal failures and problems are due to one thing: the simpletons who, with their chronic pud-pulling, have ruined themselves and destroyed all that is good and true in the cosmos. That is the true nature of this insult: the idea that everyone in the world is a wanker and that all their endeavors are semen-soaked failures. The only way out of it is to say "malaka" over and over again, to denounce anything you encounter as "malachies"; it is the universal insult that attacks the entire planet in one breath.

Very handy, that word. It is the Platonic ideal of insults.

Of course, there are times in a man's life when he doesn't need to damn the entire universe to an eternity of slack-jawed yankin'. We all regularly confront a wide spectrum of idiocy; therefore, a man should have an arsenal of many different flavors of insults. This book will inspire you, leading you on a journey through a representative handful of the millions of curses a fellow might find appropriate in any given situation.

We've tried to be selective. Anyone can attach one of George Carlin's seven dirty words as a prefix to "head" and be well served for traffic jams, under-the-breath muttering, and faux-insulting greetings to friends. But there are moments when something a bit meatier is called for. Insults for the workplace differ from those best used in a locker room, and neither would make much sense in a chess tournament. ("Nerd!" "Yes, I know. Do you know where you are, sir?") Insulting someone's mother rarely works on orphans. In today's crazy world, we simply need a full bandolier of insults.

But . . . do we? Do we really need insults at all? Aren't insults just the precinct of the desperate or powerless, or simply of people too dim-witted to make cogent and logical arguments? Isn't the whole phenomenon of insults, and indeed this very volume, a sign of the general coarsening of culture? Such concerns are shared by many people, all of them asswipes. The insult is an *ancient tradition*— multiple competing ancient traditions, actually— that we will also explore in these pages. From the poets of imperial Rome to the snarky mouth of Nobel Prize–winning statesman Winston Churchill, men have insulted one another (and the occasional lady) since the dawn of history. Perhaps even earlier.

We're the Insulting Ape. Insults, I submit to you, were the evolutionary adaptation that gave us an outlet for our anger that was cleaner than flinging feces at one another. A few million years of verbal dexterity later and, boom, the very civilization you are a part of. Yes, every aspect of this civilization is controlled and maintained by mentally defective masturbators. But what are you going to do?

Motivate the world to improve by insulting the hell out of it, that's what.

Chapter 1

Insulting Someone's Intelligence

There's an inherent difficulty in insulting a stupid man: He might just be so stupid he won't even understand that he's being insulted. Nothing's worse than insulting some water-headed baboon only to have him respond by patting you on the back and saying, "Haw haw, good one." Perhaps you've done that yourself. No, I'm just kidding. *You're* really smart. You have brains you've never even used yet.

The trick to insulting someone's intelligence is to save your insult for a smart person who's made a stupid mistake. That way, he'll get what you're saying and possibly even grudgingly acknowledge its truth, being so chagrined at his lapse of brain function. The added advantage is, when someone *really* smart says something *really* dumb—particularly in a public forum—your insult doesn't even have to be vicious to be brutally funny. Try: "Thank you. We're all refreshed and challenged by your unique point of view." Ouch.

(For a true drool-cup case, just tell him he has a small penis or something; see Chapter 3, "Insulting Someone's Sexual Prowess." If you feel you absolutely must insult an actual Pinhead American for his low intelligence, best to do so after he's left the room. Few things are more dangerous than a furious moron.)

I'm glad to see you're not letting your education get in the way of your ignorance.

———

You'd need twice the brains to qualify as a half-wit.

———

Hang on, let me look at my watch. I want to see if you can keep an idea in your head for more than thirty seconds.

———

What you lack in intelligence, you more than make up for in stupidity. (Or, *a slightly elevated version:* Your intelligence is exceeded only by your lack thereof.)

———

You're nobody's fool. Let's see if we can get someone to adopt you.

———

Is there someone else I can talk to about this? Your helper monkey, perhaps?

You're so dense, light bends around you.

———

I don't know what makes you so stupid, but whatever it is, it's really working.

———

The wheel is spinning, but the hamster is dead.

———

I refuse to enter a battle of wits with an unarmed man. (*This is also a decent comeback, especially if he didn't get the first insult you tossed his way.*)

———

You're so stupid, you tripped over the cord of your cell phone.

———

You're so slow, it takes you an hour and a half to watch *Sixty Minutes*.

———

I'd like to see things from your point of view, but I can't seem to get my head that far up my ass.

Classic Smackdowns

"A brain of feathers, and a heart of lead."
>—*Alexander Pope*

"You couldn't pour piss out of a boot if the instructions were written on the heel."
>—*Traditional Southern American insult*

"He may look like an idiot and talk like an idiot, but don't let that fool you. He really is an idiot."
>—*Groucho Marx (also swiped by the Joker in the video game* Batman: Arkham Asylum*)*

"Poor George. He can't help it. He was born with a silver foot in his mouth."
>—*Ann Richards on George H. W. Bush, at the 1988 Democratic National Convention*

"I would not want Carter and his men put in charge of snake control in Ireland."
>—*Eugene McCarthy on President Jimmy Carter*

"Dan Quayle is more stupid than Ronald Reagan put together."
>   —Matt Groening

"He's as thick as a bull's walt."
>   —Traditional Irish insult (Walt means "penis." Sorry, Walt.)

"As thick as manure and only half as useful."
>   —Another traditional Irish insult (Sensing a theme here?)

"Why do you sit there looking like an envelope without any address on it?"
>   —Mark Twain

"Sharp as a sack of wet mice."
>   —Foghorn Leghorn

"He was distinguished for ignorance, for he had only one idea and that was wrong."
>   —Benjamin Disraeli

That's Of-fun-sive!

Did you know that many of the basic insults of intelligence used to be legitimate scientific terms? Sadly, when the rest of us started saying these terms in general conversation, psychologists stopped using them in their practice. Now idiots will never know that with hard work and dedicated study they can move on up to moron status.

IQ	TERM
70–80	Borderline deficient
50–69	Moron
20–49	Imbecile
<20	Idiot

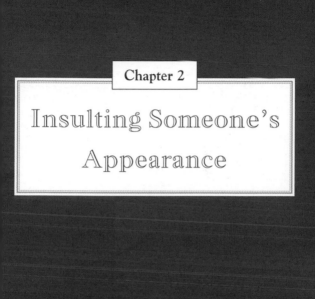

Chapter 2

Insulting Someone's Appearance

They say that a negative attitude toward overweight people is the last acceptable prejudice, but that's clearly not true. For the ugly will always be with us, and they will always be ripe for attack. Not so the obese—eventually they'll just outnumber the rest of us and, through pure social power—plus subsidies from Big Corn—will rule the world. In the same way the GLBT community reclaimed the word *queer*, the overweight will probably one day manage to reclaim *fatso* or even *oinker*. But activism goes only so far, and nobody is going to ever get up early on election day to Vote Ugly. And here's a little secret: The greatest thing about appearance, particularly for those who'd like to insult it, is that *everyone is ugly if you look hard enough*.[1]

Thin? Whatev', Karen Carpenter. A studly bodybuilder? So, how exactly do you reach your groin in the shower? Nobody can effectively rebut an insult about their appearance, because it's impossible to do so without sounding like either

---

[1] By the same token, everyone is beautiful if you look hard enough. But this is a book of insults.

a conceited ass or a crybaby. Few men are going to risk sounding lame by saying, "Nuh-uh!" to an onslaught of insults about their looks. And calling women ugly, if that's your cruel sadistic, thing, is certainly easy enough to do if you don't mind the crushing loneliness of celibacy.

Even the stars of Hollywood are horrifying demihumans once the makeup and Photoshop are taken away. If you don't believe me, just check the magazines at the cashier next time you're in the grocery store. All the top photographers know that the words "Megan Fox" rhyme with "sasquatch" for a reason.

You look like a million—every year of it.

You're so ugly, Archimedes invented the lever to push you away from him.

Look, everyone has the right to be ugly, but you're abusing the privilege.

You were so ugly at birth, your parents named you Shit Happens.

I know you're trying to insult me, but I can tell you like me. I can see your tail wagging.

Yeah, you're a real lady-killer. Mostly thanks to shock when they get a look at you.

As a baby, did you have to get your mother drunk just to breast-feed?

I don't want you to turn the other cheek; it's just as ugly.

———

Forget leaving a ring in the bathtub, you left one on the mirror.

———

You're so ugly you couldn't hail a bus.

———

If my dog's face looked like your face, I'd shave his ass and make him walk backward.

———

Wow, you look like a movie star . . . specifically, Gollum.

Celebrity Reactions to the Ugly

"Her face was her chaperone."
—*Rupert Hughes*

"She resembles the Venus de Milo: She is very old, has no teeth, and has white spots on her yellow skin."
—*Heinrich Heine*

"Oh my God, look at you. Was anyone else hurt in the accident?"
—*Don Rickles*

"Arnold Schwarzenegger looks like a condom full of walnuts."
—*Clive James*

"Sometimes she looks like a primary schoolgirl and sometimes a pensioner going shopping."
—*North Korean Foreign Ministry, on Secretary of State Hillary Clinton (By the way, how would a North Korean know what a person shopping looks like?)*

"A sail! A sail!"
> —Romeo, on spotting the dress of Juliet's nurse, Romeo and Juliet, Act II, scene 4. (She was big. Real big.)

"Campaigner Gonzalo Otalora admits he was and is no oil painting."
> —BBC.com caption on the photo of the author of Feo ("Ugly"), who has demanded that the government of his home country of Argentina tax the attractive to subsidize the ugly

"Hawaii is the only country where the Hawaiian shirts come in S, M, L, XL, Rush, and Sumo."
> —Roger Ebert on Rush Limbaugh

"She was a curious woman, whose dresses always looked as if they had been designed in a rage and put on in a tempest."
> —Oscar Wilde in The Picture of Dorian Gray

"She got her good looks from her father. He's a plastic surgeon."
> —Henny Youngman.

"He has most unwarrantably abused the privilege which all politicians have of being ugly."
—The Houston Chronicle, *on the visage of Abraham Lincoln*

"Joe Frazier is so ugly, he should donate his face to the U.S. Bureau of Wildlife."
—*Muhammad Ali*

"He now looks like a Barbie doll that has been whittled at by a malicious brother."
—*journalist Thomas Sutcliffe on early-1990s era Michael Jackson*

"You should be women, and yet your beards forbid me to interpret that you are so."
—*Banquo to the witches in* Macbeth
(P.S.: The play doesn't end well for Banquo.)

"Some women hold up dresses that are so ugly, and they always say the same thing: 'This looks much better on.' On what? On fire?"
—*Rita Rudner*

"I was such an ugly baby, my mother never breastfed me. She told me that she only liked me as a friend."

—*Rodney Dangerfield*

"Never hung poison on a fouler toad. / Out of my sight! Thou dost infect mine eyes."

—*Anne, to Richard, Richard III, Act I, Scene 2*

"Beauty is only skin deep, but ugly goes clean to the bone."

—*Dorothy Parker*

Chapter 3

Insulting Someone's Sexual Prowess

Perhaps it's because we've all grown up in a sexist, homophobic patriarchy, but few insults are harsher than those leveled against one's sexual prowess, virility (closely related to penis size, which does matter, if only psychologically), and sexuality itself. In traditional cultures, witches were often accused of stealing men's penises, and men would actually suffer from the delusion that their penises are gone. Seems silly now, but it pays to remember that at the dawn of human history, insults and supernatural curses were one and the same.[2] Think about it, dickless.

Even in societies where casual male homosexuality was tolerated or even expected, the passive homosexual role was the cause of many male anxieties. Back in ancient Greece, Aristophanes used to fling around words like *katapygnos* ("with broad buttocks") and *euryproctos* ("widened anus") in his plays; generals and politicians were often accused of being *euryprocti*, because they would do anything to succeed in the world. *Anything*.

---

[2]Explored at greater length in Chapter 5.

Seriously. They teach this stuff at Harvard.

One word of warning: Some men are extremely sensitive about their penis size. In 2010, a Miami International Airport Transportation Security Administration employee named Rolando Negrin allegedly beat a coworker with his baton (his *police* baton—he wanted to hurt the guy) after the man made fun of Negrin's penis, which had been revealed during a training session with a new whole-body image scanner. In most other life scenarios, though, small-dick jokes don't come with the added humiliation of X-ray-documented proof. So if you're willing to risk it, try taunting your sexually anxious friends with some of these:

A hard-on doesn't count as personal growth,
you know. Especially not yours.

———

Can I borrow your tweezers when you're
done masturbating?

———

You know what the only difference is between your
tiny paycheck and your tiny dick? You don't have
to beg your wife to blow your paycheck.

———

Hey, congratulations, I see the new Viagra Pez
Dispenser has your head on it.

———

With a dick that size, you'll never even be half
the man your *mother* was.

———

Save your breath—you'll need it for your
blow-up doll.

The only way you can give a woman an orgasm is by whipping out . . . your American Express card.

———

Stop trying to distract me with your nonsense and tell me what you've done with my pet gerbil.

———

You put the seat down to piss, don't you?

———

You're wearing a green hat. (This is really abusive in Mandarin Chinese; the husbands of prostitutes in China used to wear green hats, so you're basically calling someone a cuckold. Be sure to save it for your trip to China, and make sure the person you're insulting doesn't speak Cantonese or some other non-Mandarin dialect.)

———

I bet you have a really nice sports car.

Insults of the Rich and Famous

"Just how many times were you circumcised?"
>—*Jeff Foxworthy, on a conversational gambit (not) to try when seeing a man naked for the first time*

"Impotent, limp, and gutless reporters take anonymous sources and cite them as being factual references."
>—*former Alaska governor Sarah Palin, on negative press reports*

"Pamela Lee said her name is tattooed on her husband's penis. Which explains why she changed her name from Anderson to Lee."
>—*Conan O'Brien, on Tommy Lee*

"God gave men both a penis and a brain, but unfortunately not enough blood supply to run both at the same time."
>—*noted theologian Robin Williams*

"The next product I'm gonna put my name on is extra-small condoms. I can never find extra-small condoms, and I know it's really embarrassing for people—you know, from experience. Hopefully people won't be ashamed when I step forward."

> —Enrique Iglesias, *insulting his own penis, 2007*

"I said I had a small penis as a joke. And they took it literally when it is not the truth. So when people find out it's not the case, they are pleasantly surprised."

> —Enrique Iglesias, *subsequently covering up for his own penis, 2008*

"I want to show her I'm not like every other guy. Because I hate other men. When I'm f—ing you, I'm trying to f— every man who's ever f—ed you, but in his ass, so you'll say, "No one's ever done that to me in bed."

> —John Mayer, *on making love to ~~men~~ women*

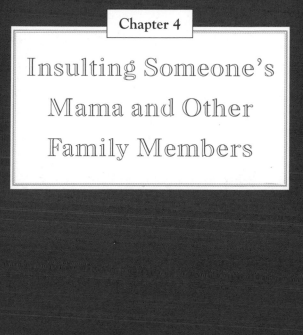

Chapter 4

Insulting Someone's Mama and Other Family Members

Ah . . . Mama. Has there even been a woman as obese, as slovenly, as imbecilic? Of course I'm referring to *your* mother, you nincompoop; *my* mother is a saint, and if you say one cross word about her, it'll be fisticuffs.

Insulting another guy's mother is an ancient tradition, but the "mama joke" in its familiar, modern form is part of the African American practice called the dozens, or snapping. Two men (usually) test their verbal skills, delivery, and timing by trading head-to-head insults about each other's mother. The dozens minimize the possibility of true violence between young men by filling in the blank after the words *your mama*—a phrase that, when uttered *alone*, means only one thing: "I've had sex with your mother." Or as Aaron in William Shakespeare's *Titus Andronicus* said, "Villain, I have done thy mother." By concentrating on the nonsexual aspects of one's opponent's mother, one can avoid the bloody fate suffered by the characters in Shakespeare's worst play.

Fat Mamas

Your mama's so fat, she sells shade.

Your mama's so fat, she's on both sides of the family.

Your mama's so fat, she bungee jumps straight to hell.

Your mama's so fat, people jog around her for exercise.

Your mama's so fat, when she has her period it looks like a murder scene. (Ew!)

Your mama's so fat, you could slap her butt and surf the waves.

Your mama's so fat, she went to the movies and sat next to everyone.

Your mama's so fat, her bra size is Parachute! (And her waist size is Equator.)

Your mama's so fat, every elevator she's on is a down elevator.

Your mama's so fat, she walked in front of the TV and I missed three commercials.

Your mama's so fat, she drives a spandex car.

Your mama's so fat, the all-you-can-eat buffet by her house had to install speed bumps.

Your mama's so fat, she sweats mayonnaise.

Your mama's so fat, when she wears a red dress, people yell, "Hey, Kool-Aid!"

Your mama's so fat that when she sued me for libel for these jokes, she went right to her attorneys, the firm of Häagen and Dazs.

Poor Mamas

Your mama's so poor, her face is on food stamps.

Your mama's so poor, she has a Dollar Meal on layaway.

Your mama's so poor, she married for the free rice.

Your mama's so poor, she can't afford to pay attention.

Your mama's so poor, when I asked her where the bathroom was she said, "Pick a corner. Any corner."

Your mama's so poor, she hangs toilet paper out to dry.

Your mama's so poor, she wrestles squirrels for acorns.

Your mama's so poor that when I saw her hobbling down the street on one shoe, I asked her, "Lose a shoe?" and she said, "Nope, just found one!"

Your mama's so poor, she has to wear her McDonald's uniform to weddings and funerals.

Your mama's so poor, her doormat doesn't say "Welcome," it says "Welfare."

Your mama's so poor, she watches her soap operas at Sears.

Your mama's so poor, the bank took her cardboard box.

Stupid Mamas

Your mama's so stupid, she got hit once by a parked car.

Your mama's so stupid, she thinks a quarterback is a refund.

Your mama's so stupid, she tried to drop acid, but the car battery landed on her foot.

Your mama's so stupid, she thought Thailand was a men's clothing store.

Your mama's so stupid, she ordered her sushi well done.

Your mama's so stupid, she thinks socialism is a way to party.

Your mama's so stupid, she filled in the emergency contact information on a job application with "911."

Ugly Mamas

Your mama's so ugly, she trick-or-treats by phone.

Your mama's so ugly, she tried to take a bath and the water jumped out.

Your mama's so ugly, even Rice Krispies won't talk to her.

Your mama's so ugly, your father takes her to work every day so he won't have to kiss her goodbye.

Your mama's so ugly, her birth certificate was an apology letter from the condom factory.

Your mama's so ugly, when she looks in the mirror her reflection pukes.

Awful Mama Potpourri

Your mama's so short, she hang glides with Doritos.

Your mama's so short, when she sits on the curb her feet dangle over the gutter.

Your mama's so old, she farts dust.

Your mama's so old, she owes Jesus five dollars.

Your mama's so old, when I told her to act her age she died.

Your mama's so old, the key on Ben Franklin's kite was to her apartment.

Your mama's so old, her birth certificate expired.

Your mama's so skinny, she uses Chapstick as deodorant.

Your mama's teeth are so rotten, when she smiles they look like dice.

Your mama's such a slut, she reminds me of a race car driver—she burns a lot of rubbers.

Your mama's such a slut, your father is a multiple-choice question.

Your mama's so bald, I can see what's on her mind.

Your mama's house is so small, we had to eat a large pizza outside.

Your mama's house is so small, when I put the key in the lock I stabbed everyone in the living room.

Your mama's got such a big mouth, she could suck an egg out of a chicken.

Your mama's glasses are so thick, when she looks at a map she can see people wave back.

Your mama's so hairy, Bigfoot took a picture of her.

Chapter 5

Insults throughout History

Let's step back for a moment.
In the beginning was not the word, but the screech
and the baring of teeth. The banging of a stick against
the ground. The beating of a chest and the flinging of
feces. But enough about your mom, let's talk insults.

Once we humans came down from the trees
and developed language, the collision of the words
shit and *head* was inevitable. But insults quickly
moved beyond the scatological as people soon
realized that with words they could create alterna-
tive realities. Today we call bad words curses, but
we also call negative wishes curses. Some of the
earliest insults are, in fact, curses in this second
sense. That is important to understand, so may
your eyes rot out of your head if you fail to read
through this section!

From *The Epic of Gilgamesh*, Enkidu to the
Harlot (Tablet VII):

> *May you never acquire anything of*
> *bright alabaster.*
> *May owls nest in the cracks of your walls.*
> *May the builder not seal the roof of your house.*

May dregs of beer stain your beautiful lap.
May a drunk soil your festal robe with vomit.

(Those last couple might seem more like the end result of a pretty good time rather than a curse, but, remember, we are speaking of the days before dry cleaning.)

Supernatural curses were also found in ancient Egypt, where the decorated the walls of tombs to warn off grave robbers and thieves. Some samples:

He shall be cooked together with the condemned.

As for anybody who shall enter this tomb in his impurity: I shall wring his neck as a bird.

His name shall not exist in the land of Egypt.

As for any man who shall destroy these, it is the god Thoth who shall destroy him.

As for him who shall destroy this inscription: He shall not reach his home. He shall not embrace his children. He shall not see success.

In Rome of the first century A.D., the poet Catullus wrote an insulting poem so foul that not until the latter half of the twentieth century did an accurate English translation appear. Even today the publisher of this book has forbidden me from providing anything more than an approximation. Enjoy the first two lines in the original Latin:

> *Pedicabo ego vos et irrumabo,*
> *Aureli pathice et cinaede Furi*

And here's a sanitized translation:

> *I will sodomize you and stick it in your face,*
> *Fellatio-loving Aurelius and catamite Furius.*

Note that Aurelius and Furius were Catullus's friends! (They'd dared to suggest that some of his previous poetry was effeminate, so he, uh, really showed them what for.) Two thousand years later, this stuff is still dangerous. In 2009 financier Mark Lowe was sued for sexual harassment, and one of the claims brought up in the course of the suit was that he responded to an e-mail that read, in part, *diligite inimicos vestros* ("love your enemy") with the first line of the poem above. "It's Catullus," he explained, "but not very polite."

The indigenous peoples of the Americas had a number of curses, too, and here we see the ancient supernatural curses moving more solidly into insult territory. It's a romantic cliché that Native Americans were nature lovers, and indeed that idea appears even in some of their insults. Common Hopi invective included stuff like "Dog lover!" and "Sheep lover!" (Though there's little hard evidence regarding which is worse. Do the dog lovers look down on the sheep lovers? I mean, dogs can bite, so you know they want it if they don't resist. But the poor sheep . . .)

A few other Native American insults:

Navaho: Go far away from me and walk around some other place!
Lakota: You, who grew up on given-away *wojapi*! (*Wojapi* is a pudding made with chokecherries or huckleberries.)
Ojibwe: Your anus!

Then there are the Brits. *The Colloquy* of Ælfric Bat, written about 1000 A.D., was a conversational manual for Anglo-Saxon speakers wishing to learn Latin. Apparently, when one lived out in the sticks, a certain type of Latin was most practical. Here's a sample of the text:

You idiot! You goat dung! Sheep dung! Horse dung! You cow dung! You pig filth! You human dung! You dog dung! Fox dung! Cat dung! Chicken droppings! You donkey dung! You fox cub of all fox cubs! You fox tail! You fox beard! You skin of a fox cub! You idiot and halfwit! You buffoon!

Quite the conversationalists, those Anglo-Saxons. But as the various non-Latin languages of Europe gained prominence, everyone got in on the nasty act. A twelfth-century traveler's guidebook written for a wealthy French person preparing for a trip to Germany offered, among other conversation gambits, this sentence, written in both High German and Latin:

Vnde ars in tine naso
Canis culum in tuo naso!

Surely, most contemporary readers can spot the word "dog"—*vnde* (hound) in German, *canis* in Latin. The whole of it says: *A dog's butt in your face!*

But it wasn't just the educational systems of the past that were vulgar and insulting; so too were the great and timeless poems of the era. Here's a snippet from Geoffrey Chaucer's *Canterbury Tales*, specifically from the Pardoner's Tale:

'I wolde I had thy coillons in myn hond
In stide of relikes or of seintuarie.
Lat kutte hem of, I wold thee help hem carie;
They shul be shryned in an hogges toord!'
This Pardoner answerde nat a word;
So wrooth was he, no word ne wolde he seye

Coillons are testicles—similar to the contemporary Spanish word *cojones*. The speaker here is telling another character that he wishes he had his balls in his hands instead of the relics he usually carries.

"Cut them off," he says, and then recommends enshrining them in a pile of pig droppings. Now that's literature!

Lest someone think society grew kinder with the Enlightenment and the arrival of modern liberal democracy, let us conclude this chapter with a few remarks from some of the founding fathers of the United States.

"The bastard brat of a Scotch peddler."
—*John Adams, on Alexander Hamilton*

"What a poor, ignorant, malicious, crapulous mass . . . "
—*John Adams, on that famed pamphlet* Common Sense *by Thomas Paine*

"A hypocrite in public life, the world will be puzzled to decide whether you are an apostate or an impostor, whether you have abandoned good principles, or whether you ever had any?"
—*Thomas Paine, on George Washington*

"His mind of that gloomy malignity which will never let him forego the opportunity of satiating it on a victim."

—*Thomas Jefferson, on Supreme Court Justice John Marshall*

"The moral character of Jefferson was repulsive. Continually puling about liberty, equality, and the degrading curse of slavery, he brought his own children to the hammer, and made money of his debaucheries."

—*Alexander Hamilton, on Thomas Jefferson*

Somehow, though, the founders did all manage to work together well enough to produce the Declaration of Independence, the Constitution, and the first several federal administrations. So maybe the problem today with Washington, D.C., *isn't* all the partisan insults. Maybe it's the endless stream of vastly insincere apologies.

That's Of-fun-sive!

Perhaps one of the glibbest political tongues of all time belonged to British prime minister Winston Churchill. A few of his zingers are classics. When Lady Astor declared, "If you were my husband, I'd poison your tea," Churchill responded, "Madam, if you were my wife, I'd drink it." (Incidentally, Astor and Churchill were both members of the Conservative Party, so one can hardly chalk up their animosity to mere partisan sniping.)

From the opposite end of the political spectrum came socialist playwright George Barnard Shaw. He reportedly sent Churchill a telegram along with two tickets to one of his plays. The telegram read: "Have reserved two tickets for opening night. Come and bring a friend—if you have one." Churchill fired back: "Impossible to come to first night. Will come to second night—if you have one." The rivalry between these two may not have been only political; both were excellent writers. Churchill even won the Nobel Prize, not for peace but for literature, in 1953. "History will be kind to me, for I intend to write it," was one of his quips on the subject. (Shaw was awarded his Nobel way back in 1925.)

Churchill supposedly let youngsters have it

as well. After having been spied leaving a washroom without washing his hands, a young man confronted Churchill: "At Eton, they taught us to wash our hands after using the toilet," he said. Unashamed, Churchill fired back: "At Harrow, they taught us not to piss on our hands."

Churchill wasn't taught everything at Harrow, though. A number of photos of the man show him flashing the V sign for victory, but with his knuckles facing the camera, which basically is a gesture meaning "Up your ass!" to many people in the United Kingdom. (See "Insulting Gestures," page 79.) The prime minister had to be tutored in the proper way to make the V-for-victory sign.

He took a few verbal losses, too. Margot Asquith, wife of Prime Minister Herbert Henry Asquith, simply declared that Churchill "would kill his own mother just so that he could use her skin to make a drum to beat his own praises." Churchill wasn't above insulting himself, either. As an old man, he responded to a woman pointing out that his fly was undone—yes, it does seem like a lot of people made a hobby of waiting for Churchill outside restrooms—with this reassuring zinger: "Madam, a dead bird won't fall out the nest."

Chapter 6

Insults at the Office

Is there anything worse than the world of work, in which you're torn from your home to be someone's servant for eight or more hours a day? And for what? Practically nothing—and then the government taxes what little money you do earn? How can anyone manage to give half their lives to such a horrifying institution? The workplace, whether farm, factory, or office, is frequently a pit of incompetence, backbiting, and authoritarian rages. You'll certainly be wanting some insults for your boss or colleagues or both—just be sure to keep these to the water cooler or locker room and away from managerial earshot. After all, you're going to need money someday to buy *Insults Every Old Man on a Fixed Income Should Know*.

He does the work of three men: Larry, Moe, and Curly.

———

She's a seagull of a manager: flies in, makes a lot of noise, shits all over everything, then leaves.

———

Diarrhea of the mouth; constipation of the ideas.

———

He's given automobile accident victims new hope for recovery. He walks, talks, performs rudimentary tasks, and can even tie a tie, all without a spine.

———

He's in his office, lost in thought. After all, it's unfamiliar territory for him.

———

I'd follow him anywhere . . . but only because he's funny to watch.

———

My supervisor would be out of her depth in a puddle.

I guess she got a concussion from bouncing her head off the glass ceiling.

———

I solved the ticket—it was a case of PEBKAC. (*That's "Problem Existing Between Keyboard and Chair." Yes, this is what the guys in the I.T. department think of you.*)

———

His machine was experiencing an I.D. Ten Type error. (*Type it out with numerals: ID10T error. That's you again.*)

———

Ah, indecision—or, as they like to call it, managerial flexibility.

———

It's good the department has learned to be cautious. Failure has taught us that much.

Professional Smack Talk

"It is very vulgar to talk about one's business. Only people like stockbrokers do that, and then merely at dinner parties."

> —*Oscar Wilde*, The Importance of Being Ernest

"You can become a Facebook Saddo."

> —*BBC Sport, forgetting to remove the placeholder text from its Olympics micro-website in 2010.*

"For example, we have a new arts series with a new presenter, not one of the silverbacks."

> —*Emma Swain, of the BBC's Knowledge Commissioning division, on the age of the network's documentary presenters*

"We can't have Woodward aborting all over the place."

> —*Abbey National banker Jonathan Nicholls, allegedly discussing a banker colleague's miscarriage (What is it with workplaces in the U.K.?)*

"OMG I HATE MY JOB!! My boss is a total pervvy wanker always making me do shit stuff just to piss me off!"

> —*a Facebook status update from a woman named Lindsay, who was quickly fired by her boss via comment. "Hi Lindsay, I guess you forgot about adding me on here?" the boss wrote in part. (Yup, the U.K. again!)*

"True confession, but I'm in one of those towns where I scratch my head and say, 'I would die if I had to live here!'"

> —*Ketchum vice president James Andrews's tweet discussing the city of Memphis, the night before giving a talk on digital media to Fedex in Memphis. The tweet was copied to Fedex marketing management in time for the morning meeting.*

"[A] coke snorting, staff-banging governor."

> —*New York State senator Kevin Parker (D) on New York governor David Paterson (D)*

"If a jet carrying [the Reverend Jesse] & Mrs. Jackson was struck by a missile and blown to smithereens that would be a tragedy . . . because it certainly wouldn't be a great loss, and it probably wouldn't be an accident either."

>*—from a wildly inappropriate "joke" email allegedly passed around by Secret Service agents, the same government office that had previously been responsible for protecting Jackson during his presidential campaigns*

"And I'm the sicko nut because I think [lesbian parents with an adopted Korean son are] about as far from what God intended a normal family to look like as giant grasshoppers playing croquet on my front lawn. But I'm the one with a screwed up view of reality."

>*—from another Secret Service work e-mail, this one putatively about going to see American Idol on tour*

That's Of-fun-sive!

As it turns out, power— even the often tiny increments of power one might wield in the workplace—does in fact corrupt. Your boss doesn't just *seem* like an incompetent jerk, he or she likely is one, thanks to psychological and even physiological changes caused by the job. Social psychologist Deborah Gruenfeld has shown empirically that when a person earns or is otherwise placed into a position of power, the "internal regulators that hold most of us back from bold or bad behavior diminish or disappear. When people feel powerful, they stop trying to 'control themselves.'"

One of Gruenfeld's studies even showed that "powerful" people working in a team would eat more than their fair share of snacks during a team meeting and were more likely to chew with their mouths open and spill crumbs all over themselves. Power may also explain why e-mails from the CEO and other top executives are often full of typos, grammatical mistakes, and meandering; it's all just a way of the CEO expressing contempt for their underlings. Bosses and managers even have higher serotonin levels than the rest of us because of the stimulus of power, according to Gruenfeld. So, hey—all the more reason to take them down a peg with a well-placed zinger or two. Plus, how can you take someone with a lapful of cookie crumbs seriously?

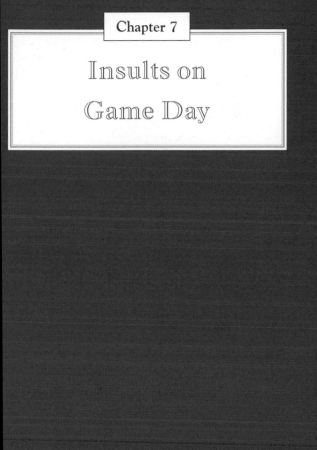

Chapter 7

Insults on
Game Day

"Do not get into any debate with a spectator about anything."

—*good advice to referees, umpires, and other officials from Alan S. Goldberger, in* Sports Officiating: A Legal Guide

Is there anything more masculine than sports? Well, maybe missing the toilet when you pee—but other than that, sports is tops. Because (a) organized sports are mostly a way to sublimate the urge to make war, and (b) the stakes on game day can be so high, it's no surprise that when men come out to play, they bring their barbed wits and potty mouths. Of course, women get into the act too, but, guys, let's own up to the trash-talking—it's not as though one often hears a contralto shout of, "Nice sequined panties, boat hips!" from the stands at a women's figure skating competition.

Sometimes, insults are integrated right into the sport; basketball is famous for trash-talking and ice hockey for chirping. In cricket, the players insult the batsman to disrupt his concentration. This ancient practice is called "sledging" and involves such immortal quips as, "Surely you're not going, doctor? There's still one stump standing," which bowler Charles Kortright said to batsman William Gilbert Grace after knocking down two of Grace's stumps. (I guarantee that this insult would be a *million* times funnier if you actually knew how the hell cricket was played.)

So here are some of the best insults for and by players—and for and by the drunks in the stands who live vicariously through the feats of world-class athletes. You know which ones will be handier for your own life, don't ya, boozy? Can you even *do* a single push-up?

What are you, sisters?!
—*great at boxing matches during an extended clinch*

Get him a bucket, he's throwin' up!
—*to pitchers in baseball*

Don't bother brushing off the corners, you're not calling them anyway!
—*for a baseball fan more discerning than the "blowing the game" guy*

Hey ref, two words: Precision Optical.
—*spectator's choice*

Hit him with your purse!
—*to any retreating fighter in combat sports*

Pardon me, sir, I believe that last call was made in error. JUST KIDDING, YOU SUCK!
—*Try it; you'll really get their attention with the first sentence.*

One fan says: Hey [name], your mom called and she said . . .
Entire home-team fan base yells: YOU SUCK!

A Quotable Roster

"Football combines the two worst features of American life: It is violence punctuated by committee meetings."
> —*conservative pundit George Will, not while at a tailgate party*

"I've seen more ice in my drink than you have all year, ya duster."
> —*classic ice hockey chirp during the face-off (A duster is a player who spends most of his time on the bench, collecting dust.)*

"I'm not the next Anna Kournikova—I want to win matches."
> —*tennis star Maria Sharapova*

"KJ Noons, attracting boos like a trailer park attracts tornados."
> —Strikeforce *play-by-play commentator Mauro Ranallo, describing the fighter's reception during his entrance*

"If they can make penicillin out of moldy bread, they can sure make something out of you."
> —*Muhammad Ali to a young boxer*

Tom Brady to Randy Moss: "You got to cut your beard." Moss to Brady: "You've got to cut your hair—you look like a girl."

> *—a 2010 altercation between New England Patriots that led to Brady refusing to throw Moss the ball in a game against the Dolphins, and which may have led to Moss being traded. (P.S. Brady says that his wife, supermodel Gisele Bündchen, loves his long hair.)*

"I'm just looking around to see who's gonna finish up second."

> *—Larry Bird again, at the three-point shooting contest at 1986's All-Star Weekend. (He won.)*

"Congratulations! Whose baby is it?"

> *—boxer Joe Frazier to Ken Norton after Norton told him, "My wife just had a baby."*

"It extremely rarely occurs to him to create something new on the chessboard."

> *—Viktor Korchnoi on Anatoly Karpov (This is considered rough stuff in chess!)*

"Hijo de puta!"

> —David Beckman to a linesman, soon after
> he began playing for Real Madrid (He
> said later that he had just heard the term
> used a lot by his teammates and had no
> idea that it meant "Son of a bitch!")

"Va te faire enculer, sale fils de pute!"

> —soccer player Nicolas Anelka to coach
> Raymond Domenech (Anelka managed
> to get himself kicked off France's World
> Cup squad when he refused to apologize
> for calling Donenech a "dirty son of a
> whore!")

"What problems do you have, apart from being
unemployed, a moron, and a dork?"

> —tennis "bad boy" John McEnroe to some
> spectator

"You can't see as well as these f—ing flowers,
and they're f—ing plastic."

> —McEnroe again, to a judge

That's Of-fun-sive!

Not only do athletes have rivalries, so too do entire sports. In recent years, mixed martial arts has been making significant inroads as a professional sport, and America's premier combat sport—boxing—has since taken a hit as audiences have grown attracted to MMA's mix of wrestling, kickboxing, and Brazilian jiu-jitsu. Increasingly it's the cage, not the ring, that proves an athlete's bad-assery. Not everyone is thrilled though:

"Everybody is different. I don't want to watch two grown men wrestling with panties on. I'm from the 'hood, we don't play that. To me, I'm not buying a ticket to watch two grown men with panties on, sweating, [with] nuts in their face. That's not me. To compare that to boxing is ludicrous. It's a porno. It's an entertainment porno. . . . I'm not wrestling a guy with panties on and his nuts in my face, and they call that a sport. I'm not criticizing people for what kind of entertainment they like. I think most of those people have chains and masks in their closets. There is something out there for everybody. I can understand if 90 percent of women were going to those things, but I can't understand a grown man sitting there with a couple of guys watching two grown men with panties on, sweating. That's just my opinion. It's not a good look."

—*boxer Bernard Hopkins, a.k.a "The Executioner," clearly just happy to be in front of a microphone for a change, on the sport of mixed martial arts*

Chapter 8

Insulting Gestures

Stammer much? Need to insult the driver of a car speeding by or the unknown person on the other end of the security camera watching your every move? Or perhaps you're in the middle of a crowded outdoor marketplace and don't want to struggle to make yourself heard but do want the vendor you're angry with to know that he has had sex with his own mother? Attend, then, as we travel the world to find some helpfully insulting gestures—though be aware that in the frantically gesturing nation of Italy, many insulting gestures are illegal if made purposefully. (Note that these laws have not reduced the frequency of insulting gestures.)

And if you're eager to insult someone in a foreign land but don't know the correct local gesture, social scientists assure us that any sort of exposure or presentation of one's buttocks is one of the few universally insulting postures.

Arab world

Showing someone the sole of your shoe is a sign of tremendous disrespect. (Remember the fellow who chucked a shoe at U.S. president George W. Bush?)

Brazil

Making the "OK" sign means, "Screw you" or "You're an asshole."

Chile

Hold palm toward sky with fingers curled to resemble a conch shell; this is a suggestion that your addressee's mother should probably wash her privates once in a while.

France

Hold one set of fingers curled and the index finger of the other hand inserted to say, "Up your ass!"

Germany

Crook and wiggle the index finger—as an American would do to gesture someone to approach—to mean, "Screw you."

Greece

The *moutza*—the display of an open palm—refers to the Byzantine practice of shoving feces in the face of criminals as they were paraded down the streets. Some also use it along with a shove to mean, "Go to hell!" One can use two palms as well.

Iran

Thumbs up is "Screw you" or, literally, "I'm going to put my thumb in your anus."

Israel

Thumbs out, like a hitchhiker signaling for a ride, is just like the Iranian version but sideways.

Japan

Four fingers thrust toward a person means, "You're four legged." Like the *moutza*, but with the thumb tucked to the palm.

North Africa

Touching or presenting anything with the left hand, which is the hand used for personal hygiene purposes, is considered utterly unclean.

Russia

The "fig" constitutes putting one's thumb between the first two fingers in a clenched fist—yet another "screw you" symbol, with a special emphasis on sexual submission.

Spain

Showing "horns," with index and pinky fingers up, other fingers held down by the thumb, means, "Your wife sleeps around." (Also effective in Italy, Portugal, and Malta.)

Saudi Arabia

Extend the left forefinger, the web of the right thumb and forefinger atop it, to say, "I'll ride you like a donkey." (Be sure to use the left hand to symbolize the donkey.)

United Kingdom

The V sign, with knuckles pointing toward target, means, "Up your ass!" Two fingers make it especially painful, you see. Other sources suggest that the two fingers are supposed to be the legs of an upside-down woman, and some folks in the U.K. do tend to flick their tongue while making this gesture. Still other sources suggest the sign comes from the rivalry between British and French archers. At any rate it's nasty, so be sure to practice it in the mirror before your trip to visit the Queen.

That's Of-fun-sive!

Many gestures that are entirely innocent in one country convey a ferocious insult in others. And some gestures imbued with international currency, such as *bras d'honneur*— or, as you probably know it, the "up yours" motion. One arm is presented while the palm of the other hand is slapped into the elbow, so the fist and forearm fly to a vertical position. It's rude in France, where the name comes from, but it's also used elsewhere. In Italy it's called the "umbrella" gesture and means, "I'll fist you with my entire forearm." In Brazil it's the "banana" and means a somewhat milder, "Screw you!" In Poland, it's called *gest Kozakiewicza*, after Olympic champion vaultist Wladyslaw Kozakiewicz, who flashed the symbol to jeering crowds in Moscow during the 1980 summer Olympics. (One presumes the Russians know what it means as well.) In Mexico the gesture, called *mentada de madre*, is done one-handed, as if throwing an uppercut, and explicitly means to insult the mother of the target. In Spain, the gesture is always topped with an extended middle finger.

Likewise, the "fig" gesture (see "Russia," page 83) is widely known in southern and central Europe as well as in the Middle East. Its origin is likely ancient Greek; it retained currency in Byzantium even as it fell out of favor in the lands once held by the Western Roman Empire. The thumb between two fingers in a fist is a symbol of the vulva (and also the anus), implying that the gesture's recipient is submissive and will eagerly bend over to receive intercourse. In some parts of the Balkans, however, the "fig" is a comical gesture and the equivalent of an exaggerated shrug of the shoulders: *Beats me*. In the United States, of course, we flash the fig gesture innocently while telling toddlers, "Got your nose!"

The famous thumbs-up gesture is also a tricky one. In Japan and Germany it just means "number one"—in those countries, counting on one's fingers often starts with the thumb rather than the index finger. In Greece, Russia, Latin America, and southern (but not northern!) Italy, it means the same as the extended middle finger does in the United States: "Sit on it!"

If there is one true universal gesture, it is the "wanker"—a loose fist being pumped over the crotch. As it turns out, virtually all cultures have similar masturbatory practices, and they all think it makes sense to label compulsive masturbators as simpletons . . . and vice versa.

Chapter 9

Backhanded
Compliments

Truly devastating insults often prove sufficiently enraging to lead to fistfights, so the wan and pathetic of the world have come up with a great way to more safely insult the hulking man-beasts who so richly deserve a little derision: compliment them, but do it slant. The backhanded or left-handed compliment is crucial for when you need an extra chuckle. After all, nothing beats insulting some stooge to his face and having him cheerily thank you for it.

The outfit is extremely slimming on you. I mean, wow.

———

Are these your kids? They seem so bright!

———

You look so nice today . . . I almost didn't
recognize you.

———

It's great to finally have a conversation with
someone who doesn't feel the need to show off his
intelligence all the time.

———

Thanks for making me dinner; it's better than
hospital food.

———

You're really a nice guy. I'd even let you date my
sister, because I know you'd never get her pregnant
or anything like that . . .

———

You have the greatest amount of untapped
potential of anyone I've ever met.

You're beautiful where it counts. On the inside.

I could never pull off as much drinking as you get done in one night. It's really impressive.

You look great on that Facebook pic. Did you learn Photoshop recently?

Nice jacket; I didn't even realize that sort of thing was back in style.

You're smart. Just not book smart. Or street smart.

I really like your nails. Are they fake?

Nice wheels, bro. If anyone other than you owned it, I'd call it a penis substitute.

As it turns out, you don't match the "dumb blonde" stereotype at all. I'm pleasantly surprised.

———

Just another ten pounds and you'll be done.

———

Congrats on your new girlfriend! I'm sure this relationship will be just as successful as all your past ones.

Passive-Aggressive Zingers

"[Michele Obama] is so interesting looking and so bright. That will always take you farther. When you're a great beauty, it's always downhill for you. If you're someone like Mrs. Obama, you just get better with age."

> —*aging but still fairly attractive supermodel Iman (see what I did there?), on First Lady Michelle Obama*

"I mean, you got the first mainstream African American who is articulate and bright and clean and a nice-looking guy. I mean, that's a storybook, man."

> —*Senator Joe Biden, on Barack Obama (Obama later selected Biden as his running mate, so did the man just not get it?)*

"I think that's why Meryl Streep is working so much, because she looks like a woman we can all relate to . . . Meryl looks like an unmade bed."

> —*Sharon Stone, on superior actress Meryl Streep*

"Now, there are brilliant technicians such as James Cameron who create wizardry. But, unfortunately, content takes a back seat, as Francis Ford Coppola and Sir Richard Attenborough have said many times. Stalwarts such as John Ford, Billy Wilder, and William Wyler were not only versatile and thinking directors, they concentrated on a variety of subjects, with importance to content."

—director Martin Scorsese, on Cameron

"Joe Cole is quicker than Benayoun, but Yossi is better tactically. He understands what I tell him."

—Chelsea team manager Carlo Ancelotti, on new Chelsea footballer Yossi Benayoun

"I heard she put out a song that's about me, or about some old habits or whatever . . . I'm just stoked that she finally has a song with some substance on her record."

—Travie McCoy, responding to his ex Katy Perry's song "Circle the Drain," which allegedly contains a lyric about McCoy falling asleep during foreplay

"You have the best set of teeth I've ever seen on an inmate."

> —*a prison dentist to writer Jim Goad*

"If you were to draw a cartoon of her, you would know immediately who she is. She's an icon."

> —*Chris Linn, the executive vice president for pilots at MTV, on* The Jersey Shore's *Snooki.*

"The most common thing I hear from people who meet me is, 'Say, you're really nice.' It's a back-handed compliment, I know, but I'll take it."

> —*Hillary Clinton, realizing what people think of her on the campaign trail during the 2008 Presidential race.*

That's Of-fun-sive!

"Pick-up artists"—that is, men with low self-esteem who enjoy sleeping with women with even lower self-esteem—have perfected the "neg," or mildly negative comment. Firing a "neg" at a woman of recent acquaintance is a tactic that supposedly signals to her that she does not meet the pick-up artist's high standards. This supposedly shifts the locus of power away from the beautiful woman—who presumably is accustomed to either being complimented by men pursuing her or cruelly insulted by the men she has rejected—and toward the random douchebag who wants to lure her to bed.

So, "Nice nails, are they fake?" according to pick-up scripts, is supposed to lead to the admission, "Yes, they are," bringing the woman down a peg and thus making her more amenable to soiling herself on the idiot who's asking. Of course, most women know better than to fall for such nonsense, and will probably just fire back: "Nice package. Is that one pair of socks or two?"

Which brings us to our next chapter: *dealing* with being insulted.

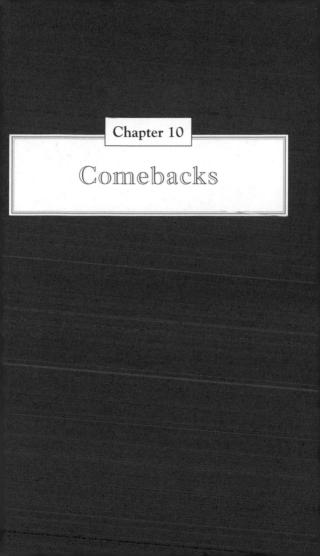

Chapter 10

Comebacks

"Why is it an insult, to be told what is self-evident?" wondered the famed Stoic philosopher Seneca. He also recommended that those who take offense at others' words consider the source; after all, most people who insult others are just overgrown children. Of course, some insults are more easily accepted than others. Being called "baldy" shouldn't really upset you that much, even if it's true. Someone pointing out that you smell like landfill is a bit tougher—*especially* if it's true. Yet still, Seneca insists "men are not harmed, only angered" by insults. And two millennia of mothers agree with him; who taught you that old saying, "Sticks and stones may break my bones, but names will never harm me?"

Yeah, well, I ain't your mama. So here's some real advice. First, don't visibly express any anger at being insulted. Seneca, the Buddha, and all those other losers were right about that much: If you start fuming or gnashing your teeth, you have already lost. Second, don't over-escalate. You'll just look like a bully in the end. Some rough parity is called for in firing off a comeback; feel free to ignore the minor insults, or come back with an equally small-stakes rejoinder. "Yeah, I'll write that down for my kids to use," will do most of the time. For stronger insults, here's a list.

Wow, that's an awesome insult. Did it come to you in a dream?

———

Who farted? Oh wait, that was you talking, wasn't it?

———

Hey, it's Koko, the ape scientists taught to speak! Not well, though.

———

Ah, you want some attention. Very good, I can do that. Let me just start tweeting all of these for you. At-sign dumbass, right?

———

It's all right, it's all right. Let's have a hug.
(*If you know any judo, this is doubly good once you get a grip on him.*)

———

That reminds me of the other day, when I was having sex with your wife…

If I throw a stick, will you leave?

———

Are you always an idiot, or is this some sort of
special show for me?

———

Usually, I'm an eye-for-an-eye, tooth-for-a-tooth kind
of guy, but given the looks of that mouth, I'll pass.

Comebacks to Remember

"Just think: the only laugh that man will probably ever get is for stripping and showing off his shortcomings."

> —*David Niven, on the streaker who interrupted him during the 1973 Academy Awards*

"You lose."

> —*Calvin Coolidge to (supposedly) Dorothy Parker, who told the president, "Mr. Coolidge, I've made a bet against a fellow who said it was impossible to get more than two words out of you."*

"My friend, we don't support savages, we just allow them to come to our meetings."

> —*British Prime Minister Harold Wilson, responding to the shouted demand that he explain why he supported "savages" in Rhodesia*

"How can they tell?"

> —Parker, on Coolidge, when informed that
> Coolidge had died

"I'm Kirk Douglas's son! No, I'm Kirk Douglas's
son! I am!"

> —an entire crowd of hecklers in response
> to frustrated stand-up comedian and
> nepotism victim Eric Douglas bellowing
> at them, "I'm Kirk Douglas's son!"

That's Of-fun-sive!

You can get your fill of insults and comebacks every night of the week, as long as you can handle a two-drink minimum. (You can handle that, can't you, grandma?) Stand-up comedians face off against hecklers all over the world—thanks again mostly to that two-drink minimum. But a heckler wasn't always just some frat boy shouting, "You suck!" after his first beer; the term originally referred to flax-combers—combing flax is called heckling—in the textile trade. Radical hecklers in the United Kingdom used to break up the monotony of their jobs and win some workplace solidarity by cleverly interrupting the worker in charge of reading off the day's news and announcements. (The radicals also took their act to the street, to trade barbs with conservative politicians and bosses.)

Heckling stand-up comedians can be tricky. The comedians are pros, and audiences are usually sympathetic toward them, not toward some drunk with an insult book on his lap. So if you're going to heckle, make sure that you are loud, articulate, and funnier than the stand-up. When an overweight male comedian comes out and starts doing unfunny self-deprecating humor, for instance, you might be tempted to shout, "Show us your tits!"—but it's entirely possible that he'll whip off his shirt, come down into the audience, and give you a lap dance. Unless it's open-mic night, comedians are on stage in the first place because they're professionals at work, and most of them have many excellent rejoinders ready to smack you with at a moment's notice, from, "Hey, I remember my first beer too," to improvised humiliations aimed precisely at you and your stupid tie, your double chin, your ugly date, and your own working life, which surely involves providing brief moments of personal intimacy at the bus station for quarters.

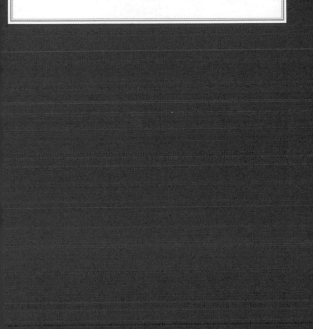

Chapter 11

Insults between Writers

Writers and other creative types don't really need any special type of insult to cover their shortcomings—pretty much any insult you would use against a poor person, an impotent loser, or anyone who still lives with their parents is likely to apply just as well to any artists or literati you encounter. Heck, you can even just dismissively ask, "How's that novel/play/painting/minimalist-opera-for-kazoo/performance-piece-where-you-shove-a-light-bulb-up-your-butt going?" and snort during the answer—that will handle everything.

But every once in a while, one of these losers will actually make good, and when they do, the claws come out on all their peers. All those years of poverty and anguish do something to an artist's soul . . . something dark. Professional writers are as mean and petty as aspiring writers are pretentious and obnoxious—mostly to one another, and they tend to be fairly quotable too. Literary insults are also handy for the rest of us; during a cocktail party, rattling off a famous putdown of Henry James or Mark Twain certainly beats admitting, "Uh, I never really read that author." (Another cocktail party tip: If asked what the last book you've read was, for the love of God, don't mention this one!) So come along, won't you, on a magical journey to the land where artsy meets fartsy?

"Poor Faulkner. Does he really think big emotions come from big words?"
> —*Ernest Hemingway, on fellow modernist William Faulkner*

"He has never been known to use a word that might send a reader to the dictionary."
> —*William Faulkner, on Ernest Hemingway*

"Have you ever heard of anyone who drank while he worked? You're thinking of Faulkner. He does sometimes—and I can tell right in the middle of a page when he's had his first one."
> —*Ernest Hemingway, on William Faulkner*

"A hack writer who would not have been considered fourth rate in Europe, who tricked out a few of the old proven sure-fire literary skeletons with sufficient local color to intrigue the superficial and the lazy."
> —*William Faulkner, on Mark Twain*

"I often want to criticize Jane Austen, but her books madden me so that I can't conceal my frenzy from the reader; and therefore I have to stop every time I begin. Every time I read *Pride and Prejudice* I want to dig her up and beat her over the skull with her own shin bone."

> —Mark Twain, on Jane Austen (*try this one out on dates!*)

"I don't think Robert Browning was very good in bed. His wife probably didn't care for him very much. He snored and had fantasies about twelve-year-old girls."

> —W. H. Auden, on Robert Browning

"Nothing but old fags and cabbage stumps of quotations from the Bible and the rest, stewed in the juice of deliberate, journalistic dirty-mindedness—what old and hard-worked staleness, masquerading as the all-new!"

> —D. H. Lawrence, on James Joyce

"An unmanly sort of man whose love-life seems to have been largely confined to crying in laps and playing mouse."

> —W. H. Auden, on Edgar Allan Poe

"An enthusiasm for Poe is the mark of a decidedly primitive stage of reflection."

> —Henry James, on Edgar Allan Poe

"It [any novel by James] is like a church lit but without a congregation to distract you, with every light and line focused on the high altar. And on the altar, very reverently placed, intensely there, is a dead kitten, an egg-shell, a bit of string. . . . "
    —H. G. Wells, on Henry James

"There are two ways of disliking poetry. One way is to dislike it; the other is to read Pope."
    —Oscar Wilde, on Alexander Pope

"Am reading more of Oscar Wilde. What a tiresome, affected sod."
    —Noel Coward, on Oscar Wilde

"I'm sure the poor woman meant well, but I wish she'd stick to re-creating the glory that was Greece and not muck about with dear old modern homos."
    —Noel Coward, on Mary Renault

"He would not blow his nose without moralizing on the conditions in the handkerchief industry."
    —Cyrill Connolly, on George Orwell

"You see people reading him on airplanes, the same people who are reading John Grisham, for Christ's sake."

—*John Irving, on Tom Wolfe*

"I think he was mentally defective."

—*Evelyn Waugh, on Marcel Proust*

"That's not writing; that's typing."

—*Truman Capote, on Jack Kerouac*

"He's a fine writer, but I wouldn't want to shake hands with him."

—*Jacqueline Susann, on Philip Roth,*
author of the masturbation classic
Portnoy's Complaint

"Such writing is a sort of mental masturbation. . . . I don't mean that he is indecent but viciously soliciting his own ideas into a state which is neither poetry nor anything else but a Bedlam vision produced by raw pork and opium."

—*Lord Byron on John Keats* (Author's note: I really wanted to call this book "Raw Pork and Opium.")

Chapter 12

Obscure Insults

Back in the days before men were as coarse as we are today, when we still tried to avoid using the roughest of vulgar curse words in proper society, endless numbers of "polite" insults were in common usage, offering a robust selection for every occasion and for every simpleton one might encounter. We still hear some of these words today, at least on network television during daytime hours or from hopeless eccentrics of the sort one meets early in the morning on undertrafficked subway platforms. But honestly, how many people can still keep their ninnies straight from their nincompoops? After this chapter, you'll be one of them.[3]

aeolist: a "windy" talker who pretends to be artistically inspired but accomplishes nothing

bissigen: to insult

cacafeugo: Spanish for "shitfire," or someone who brags and mouths off constantly

clodpate: fool

---

[3] Yes, that was deliberately ambiguous.

cronk: to positively burst with insults against others

dag: Australian for "nerd"

dasypygal: hairy-assed

dunderwhelp: an idiot, especially a young one

ephemeromorph: a form of life too low to be considered either animal or vegetable (This word is a scientific term and not an insult per se, but together, dear readers, we can make it happen!)

FIB: pronounced "fib," an acronym for f—ing Illinois bastard, an insult that Wisconsites use to refer to Illinoisans when they aren't around (Most people from Illinois have never heard of it.)

fireship: a woman, generally a whore, who spreads venereal disease

franion: a loose woman, or a very silly man

gunsel: passive homosexual, later transformed by author Dashiel Hammett in *The Maltese Falcon* into a word for a gun-carrying criminal to get it past the editors of the pulp-fiction magazine *Black Mask*

guttersnipe: a homeless child

hircine: smelling like a goat, or having goatlike attributes

his nibs: U.K. term for a self-important male who is utterly insignificant

hobbledehoy: rude or clumsy, generally aimed at young men

hoyden: a thoughtless young woman, or one that lacks self-control

jack-a-lent: a simpleton; someone insignificant

jackanapes: a conceited person (Note: jacka-napes is not the plural of jackanape.)

jeeter: an uncouth and sloppy person

jobbernowl: very stupid indeed

jumentous: smelling of horse urine

knave: a dishonorable person; once literally someone of low as opposed to noble birth

labrose: fish lipped

mountebank: a charlatan

mudsill: the underclass or proletarians (like "dregs of society")

naffin: almost but not quite an idiot

napiform: turnip shaped (like your head!)

natiform: ass shaped (like your head!)

nincompoop: a fool, especially a naïve one; supposedly a combination of ninny and poop (a Dutch term for a fool)

ninny: a naïve fool (a play on "innocent")

nithin: the most cowardly and vile person imaginable

numpty: idiot (but meant in a semifriendly way)

oligophrenial: feebleminded

onkus: unpleasant or bad

pettifogger: a crooked lawyer

pill: a boring person

plug-ugly: a thug or street tough, from the infamous Baltimore gang

popinjay: a vain person or ostentatiously dressed man

puke: slang for someone from Missouri, used in the states surrounding Missouri

pukoid: ugly

quean: whore or whorish

queer plunger: a con man

rixatrix: a nasty old lady who berates others

row you up Salt River: a phrase used to threaten someone with a beating

rudesby: a boorish man

rumbelow: a street walker, a low-class prostitute

saucebox: a jackanapes

shard-born: born in a pile of crap

schlemiel: Yiddish for a clumsy person

schlimazel: Yiddish for a guy with bad luck, at least some of it deserved, though sometimes the bad luck just comes from proximity to a schlemiel

skell: a bum, a low-level criminal

slubberdegullion: a slobbering and dirty person

toerag: a bum or generally worthless person (from the use of rags in shoes rather than socks)

trollop: everyone knows this is a term for prostitute, but it was also once used for women who were unkempt or ugly or who kept a sloppy home

uphill gardener: homosexual

washitu: an ethnic slur for "white" in Lakota

wally: an idiot, or someone without common sense

Winchester goose: a spreader of venereal disease (*see* fireship)

That's Of-fun-sive!

Once again, the Bard brings us the mother lode.
In act 2, scene 2 of *King Lear*, Kent encounters
Oswald and says, "Fellow, I know thee." Then
Kent explains what he knows Oswald for:

A knave; a rascal; an eater of broken meats;
a base, proud, shallow, beggarly, three-suit-
ed, hundred-pound, filthy, worsted-stocking
knave; a lily-livered, action-taking knave, a
whoreson, glass-gazing, super-serviceable
finical rogue; one-trunk-inheriting slave;
one that wouldst be a bawd, in way of good
service, and art nothing but the composition
of a knave, beggar, coward, pandar, and the
son and heir of a mongrel bitch: one whom
I will beat into clamorous whining, if thou
deniest the least syllable of thy addition.

Some of these terms are still current, but here's
a handy guide for the rest: *Broken meats* are
scraps, so Oswald is poor. *Three-suited* means that
he has the social status of a servant, who had
three changes of clothes issued to them per year.
Hundred-pound, on the other hand, suggests that
Oswald is overpaid. Yet, he's a *worsted-stocking*

knave, meaning that he dresses informally in wool stockings instead of proper silk stockings.

An *action-taking knave* is someone who prefers litigation to fighting; someone who is always *glass-gazing* is vain. *Super-serviceable* is a toadie, someone who serves for personal gain. *Finical* we have today as "finicky," but it refers specifically to finicky about one's appearance. A *one-trunk inheriter* is, again, a poor person—the British were class conscious, after all. *Bawd* and *pandar* are terms for "pimp," and the final bit about "thy addition" refers to all these terms collectively, which Kent has granted Oswald as though they were great honors.

Chapter 13

Insults from around the World

"Insultology" probably isn't a word, but it should be one. Anthropologists are, as you read these very words, combing the world for insults—and for broad trends in insults—in global cultures. Although cultural diversity naturally yields great diversity in dirty words, verbal snipes, and blasphemies, nonetheless a certain level of universality exists across cultures, as seen in our discussion of insulting gestures (see page 79). Scatology, sexual behaviors, and identification with certain out-groups (such as a competing or minority religion) pop up time and again.

And then there is a big one: *Go have sex with your own mom.* It's sexual, it's a violation of the incest taboo, and it suggests that the would-be Lothario can't get anyone to sleep with him other than his or her own relatives. No wonder virtually every culture on earth has embraced some variation on "motherf—er" as an insult. Here are some favorites from around the world.

Arabic

Your mother banged your father in the ass so much that he got pregnant and held you in his balls.

Mandarin Chinese

Screw your mother.
Screw your elder uncle.
Screw your ancestors for eighteen generations back.

Turco-Mongolian

I urinate on your father's head and have intercourse with your mother. (Note the variation: *He's* doing your mom, not saying that you do.)

Greek

Screw the Mother of God. (If my father is any guide, this one is often directed at recalcitrant lawnmowers.)

But there is more to the world of insults than sex with your mom. Here are a selection of unusual insults and bizarre slams from many languages, with translations and helpful commentary.

Afrikaans

dom doos: You are a dumb pussy.

Armenian

Peranuht shoonuhe cockne: The dog should poop on you.

Canadian

goof: In prison culture in Canada, this otherwise innocuous term refers to child molesters who like to rape young boys. It's often open season on goofs in Canadian prisons, so calling a fellow inmate a goof will almost invariably lead to a fight. In parts of Hamilton, Ontario, it's a fighting word outside prison as well.

Dutch

kankerlijer: cancer sufferer

kanker hoer: cancer whore (disease is a significant locus of insults in Dutch)

je moeder: your mama

Finnish

Vedä päähäs: Pull it over your head. ("It" being either a vagina or an anus—basically, go screw yourself.)

French

biloute: small dicked (Northern dialect)

Faut péter dans l'eau pour faire des bulles: Go fart in the water and make bubbles.

Je te pisse en zig-zags au raie de cul: I piss in zigzags across the crack of your ass.

Merde puissance treize: Shit to the thirteenth power. (This one is actually a public service. Other references may list this phrase as an insult or exclamation, but in fact it's a way of wishing someone good luck.)

Mes couilles sur ton nez: My balls on your nose.

Retourne enculer les mouches: Go screw flies. (Rough language, but it's fairly mild—it's an insulting way of telling someone that they like to split hairs in an argument.)

French Canadian

tête carré: square-head (derogatory term for Anglophones)

German

Arschgeige: ass-violin ("dipshit")

Depp: idiot. (Don't tell Johnny.)

Du hast ja wohl den Arsch offen?: Is your ass open? ("What the hell is wrong with you?")

Hosenscheisser: short-pant shitter ("Coward.")

Sitzpinkler: one who urinates sitting down ("Wimp.")

Warmduscher: warm showerer ("Wimp" again— real men take *cold* showers.)

Hindi

chutiya: vile person

randwa: man-whore

Sala: brother-in-law (When used as a proper noun, it implies that you slept with the

target man's sister, and is considered a
ferocious insult.)

Japanese

kusatta gaijin: stinking foreigner

Regee no ojisan: Uncle Reggae (a homeless
person with dirty, matted hair; not an
ethnically sensitive insult)

takenoko-zoku: bamboo-shoot youth (Comes
from a greaser/rockabilly-type scene that
sprung up suddenly, like bamboo shoots, in
the streets of Harajuku. Similar to "chav"
in England with its suggestion of low-class
and criminality.)

Zurui chibi: sneaky dwarf

Klingon

Hab Sosli Quch: Your mother has a smooth
forehead! (Clearly, this one doesn't work
on Captain Kirk–era Klingons.)

Korean

go-ja: a penisless man.

kotchu sekki: son of a penis

knee be she be peck pojie da: Your mother has bald genitals. ("Your mother is a whore," basically; in Korea, pubic hair is heavily associated with fertility and desirable sexual partners.)

Norwegian

hæstkuk: horse-cock (similar to "asshole")

Svarte faen: black devil (A lot of Northern European insults are mild, and many involve Satan somehow.)

Polish

pierdolic: to fuck (Handily, this word is incredibly versatile in Polish, just as it is in English.)

Scottish

fannybaws: an unpleasant or ineffectual person (From fanny, meaning "vagina," and baws, for "testicles.")

Serbian

Da bog da trazio detzoo Gaygerovim broyachem:
   May God make it so you search for your
   children with a Geiger counter.

Da bog da ti kuca bila na CNN-U: May your
   house be live on CNN. (Seriously, the
   Serbians have dragged traditional insults
   kicking and screaming into the 21st
   century.)

Spanish

Chupamela!: Suck it!

hijo de mil putas: son of a thousand bitches

me cago en la hostia: I defecate in the
   Communion Host ("Goddamn it.")

meado por los gatos: pissed on by all the cats
   (Argentine slang)

Swahili

Kenyan Kisw: someone who thinks in English
   and then translates his thoughts into
   Swahili

Mtasha: proud, arrogant (also a term for a

white foreigner)

Utalijua Jiji: You will face the city. (meaning, an incompetent person who needs help from others)

Turkish

Ebenin amına koyim—I'll put this in your midwife's vagina.

Walloon

u pus l'sindge mont waut, au pus qu'on vwè qu's'cou è pèlé: The higher the monkey climbs, the more you can see its scabby ass. (For social climbers and brown-nosers in the workplace.)

Hungary

agyilag zokni: mental sock ("idiot")

Az Isten faszát!: The Lord's penis! (a generalized expletive)

fapicsa: wooden vagina ("frigid woman")

Maldives

"Before buggering a chicken, check if the hole is clean. That is because the people of the countries that you are from are familiar with the taste of the holes of chicken." (From a fake "traditional Maldivian" ceremony conducted in Dhivehi in 2010 for a Swiss couple who did not speak the language.)

That's Of-fun-sive!

Here's a foreign phrase for you: *Lèse majesté*, or "insult to majesty." Lèse majesté is the crime of insulting a sovereign or the state itself. During the era of powerful monarchies, insults against a king or emperor were harshly punished, and even today there are places where lèse majesté is a crime.

In Thailand, for example, insulting King Bhumibol can be punished by up to fifteen years in prison. And since the king is the living avatar of the state, any individual can go to the police and file a complaint against anyone else. Furthermore, repeating the insult is itself considered insulting, so the press cannot completely describe the supposed attacks on royalty dignity. An act as simple as refusing to stand during the playing of the Thai national anthem can bring charges of lèse majesté, so forget about denouncing Bhumibol as an *ai gaae dtan haa glap*—a senile man who has forgotten everything except his desire for sex. (In 2005, the king publicly declared himself open to criticism, but as the law remains on the books and available to all, it is still used as a political weapon.)

In many European countries as well, lèse majesté is still on the books. In Spain in 2007, two cartoonists were fined 3000 euros each for their cartoon of Crown Prince Felipe and his wife, Letizia, having sex, which appeared on the cover of the satirical magazine *El Jueves*. In the Netherlands, a man was fined 400 euros for calling Queen Beatrix a whore in front of a police officer. In Poland, even foreign heads of state enjoy the privilege of lèse majesté: Human rights activists were arrested in 2005 for protesting Russian president Vladimir Putin. The next year, a man named Hubert Hoffman was arrested at a Warsaw train station and complained that President Lech Kaczynski and his twin brother, Jaroslaw, were transforming Poland back into a Communist dictatorship. When the police told him to be respectful of the president, Hoffman farted and was immediately arrested for showing contempt for the president. Hoffman then jumped bail, and a nationwide manhunt ensued.

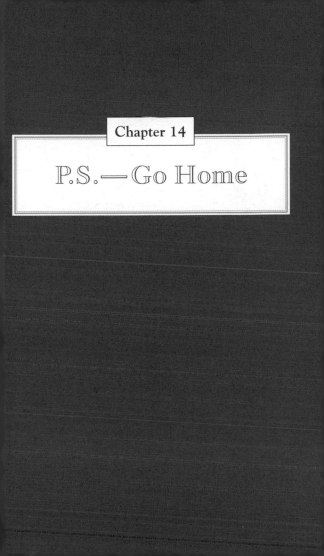

Chapter 14

P.S.—Go Home

Do civilized men even need insults? Wouldn't the world be a better place if we lived up to our aspirations rather than living down to our urges? Rather than wasting our time reading lists of insults, shouldn't we be seeking enlightenment in books of wisdom and insight? The answers to these questions are yes, no, and sometimes.

Ultimately, humanity needs insults. We learn and thrive on conflict and competition, but we also benefit from cooperation and community. Insults are guideposts for both these aspects of the human life: a well-timed *bon mot* can rob a petty tyrant of his power, if even just for a moment. (There's a reason poets are often the first arrested after a coup.) Insults can also help form bonds of solidarity, as can be seen in the reclaiming of words like *queer*. Even the political terms *Tory* and *Whig* started out as insults that were ultimately appropriated by their targets.

That being said, this book is not a tool to help you perfect the power of the insult—do your own dirty work, you cretin. No, my only hope is that this little tome helped you get through your day, and that if you decide to share a sharp line or two with a buddy, you'll both smile.

Well, actually, I do have a second hope. I hope none of you get the bright idea to e-mail me with some extra insults you found on Google that you think I might need for the sequel. Okay? Now go on—beat it, you malaka.

Acknowledgments

I'd like to thank the Internet, which makes all things possible.